The Very First EASTER

PAUL L. MAIER
ILLUSTRATED BY FRANCISCO ORDAZ

CONCORDIA PUBLISHING HOUSE · SAINT LOUIS

6   7   8   9   10   12   11   10   09   08   07   06

Easter books for children often focus on the delights of spring or bunnies, colored eggs, and chocolate candies in an Easter basket. And why not? Nature coming back to life has been celebrated ever since early pagans named their April fertility festival in honor of Eostre, the Anglo-Saxon goddess of spring—thus the name Easter. However, because the resurrection of Jesus also happened at the same time of year, Easter took on a profoundly sacred significance, which is too often missing in literature for the young.

These pages return the sacred dimension to Easter. As in the companion book, *The Very First Christmas*, the setting is America's western mountains where a forest ranger and his wife tell their bright ten-year-old son about the ministry, trial, death, and resurrection of Jesus. Their secluded location has prevented the young man from attending Sunday school regularly. In this book, his parents answer the questions he—and perhaps many like him—have about "the *very first* Easter."

Some vocabulary or events may be beyond the understanding of your child. Take time to explain them and share the story of your own faith as, together, you read about "the *very first* Easter."

Paul L. Maier

Christopher sat at the kitchen table, dyeing Easter eggs. "I just *love* this time of year, especially the jelly beans and chocolate rabbits," he said. "Remember when I used to believe in the Easter bunny? You know, some kids at school say he's a myth—whatever that is."

"A myth? Well, that's like a fairy tale," said Mom, smiling.

"Remember, Mom? I don't *like* fairy tales anymore," Chris sighed.

"Oh, that's right. You want only *true* stories—like the one I told you about the birth of Jesus." Mom rescued several eggs from getting dyed to death, then her face brightened with an idea.

"Chris, why don't we read the *true* story about the *very first* Easter?" Mom asked. "It's much more important than the Easter bunny, colored eggs, or even jelly beans."

"Splendid idea, dear!" Christopher's father said as he walked into the kitchen.

"Hi, Dad!" said Chris. "Hey, you used to be a teacher. Maybe *you* should tell me about Easter instead of Mom."

"Okay," Dad agreed as he sat down next to Chris. "Since Easter is next week, let's read about it tonight."

That night after supper, they sat down for evening devotions. "Chris, this has been called 'The Greatest Story Ever Told,' " Dad began. "Do you remember how you and your mom read from the gospel of St. Luke to learn more about the birth of Jesus?"

"Sure! But I read more of it than Mom did!"

"Good for you! Well, let's continue reading from Luke." Dad reached for the family Bible, opened it, and pointed to a verse that Chris read aloud.

And Jesus grew in wisdom and stature, and in favor with God and men. (Luke 2:52)

"Jesus grew up in Galilee," Dad explained. "He began His marvelous ministry there and called 12 men to be His disciples, or students. They followed Jesus around and learned from Him. He taught thousands of people in the hills and valleys, at the seashore, and in villages and towns. Jesus' words showed people the way to God— the God who loved them enough to come down to their level in that very extraordinary man who was speaking to them."

"How do we know Jesus was really God?" asked Chris.

"Jesus spoke the truth as only God could. And He did incredible miracles. He gave hearing to the deaf and sight to the blind. He cured the sick and made the lame walk. He even stopped the wind and calmed the waves. Only *God* could do those things."

Chris nodded slowly. Dad read several familiar accounts from Luke, then added, "Jesus even raised the dead. Once when He was visiting a small town called Nain, Jesus saw a young man being carried out for burial. He comforted the man's mother who was crying. Here, Chris, read what Jesus said."

"Young man, I say to you, get up!" The dead man sat up and began to talk, and Jesus gave him back to his mother. (Luke 7:14b–15)

"Cool!" Chris exclaimed. "I wish I could have seen that! But why did Jesus let him die in the first place? Couldn't He have gotten there earlier and kept him from dying?"

"Of course!" Mom joined in. "But because of this miracle we can know that we don't have to be afraid to die because Jesus, as God, has power even over death."

"The teaching, preaching, and healing ministry of Jesus lasted for about three years," Dad continued. "Then Jesus knew the time had come to finish the glorious task for which He had been born. The greatest events in His ministry would happen during Holy Week—the week that changed the world.

"It was a Sunday in spring," Dad began. "Many people had come to Jerusalem to celebrate the Passover, the annual festival held to remember how God had freed His people from slavery in Egypt.

"Jesus already knew what was going to happen later during that momentous week, He decided not to slip into Jerusalem unnoticed. He rode into the city on the back of a donkey in what became a big parade, with cheering crowds waving palm branches along the sides of the road. That's why it's called Palm Sunday. Read on, Chris."

The whole crowd of disciples began joyfully to praise God in loud voices for all the miracles they had seen: "Blessed is the King who comes in the name of the Lord." (Luke 19:37b–38a)

Chris looked up and said, "I can understand why they cheered and called Jesus a king and all, but a king should ride in a royal chariot, not on a *donkey*!"

"The past was important to these people, Chris. They lived their history," Dad explained. "You see, many years earlier, King David had entered Jerusalem in triumph riding a donkey, not a chariot. The donkey was like a royal carriage to these people."

"Kind of like a limo," Chris announced. "So did they crown Jesus?"

"No," said Dad. "Some religious leaders didn't like Jesus and called Him a false prophet, a fake Messiah. The Messiah would be God's great prophet, priest, and king as foretold in Old Testament times. Jesus *was* that Messiah, but His enemies didn't believe it."

"After all those miracles, why not?" Chris asked.

"They said Jesus performed the miracles with help from the devil, not God."

"*What?*" Chris exclaimed. "That doesn't make sense! The devil does bad things, not good ones."

"But they didn't believe Jesus was God," Dad explained. "Some of the religious leaders despised Jesus because He often challenged them and the things they did. One example is the day after Palm Sunday, when Jesus chased merchants and bankers out of the temple, even though the religious leaders had let them do business there."

"Then what happened?" asked Chris.

"Well, it was the Thursday after Palm Sunday. Jesus had been staying in Bethany at the home of His friends Mary, Martha, and Lazarus. That evening, He and His disciples went into Jerusalem. They gathered in an upstairs room to eat their Passover dinner. Then Jesus did something that made this Passover dinner different. Go ahead and read, Chris."

And [Jesus] took bread, gave thanks and broke it, and gave it to them, saying, "This is my body given for you; do this in remembrance of me." In the same way, after the supper He took the cup, saying, "This cup is the new covenant in my blood, which is poured out for you." (Luke 22:19–20)

Chris stopped reading. "Haven't I heard those words before?"

"Yes, you have. That was the beginning of the longest meal in history," Dad said.

"Come on, Dad! What do you mean?"

"What we call the Lord's Supper or Holy Communion was started that night and it continues to be celebrated throughout the world today. Jesus said, 'Do this in memory of me.' Believers who eat the bread and drink the wine receive the body and blood of Christ and remember all He did to win our salvation. The Lord's Supper is called a sacrament—something through which God offers His grace and grants forgiveness of sins."

Then Dad added, "Remember those men who didn't like Jesus and were trying to get rid of Him? Read the words of Jesus in the very next verse."

"But the hand of him who is going to betray me is with mine on the table." (Luke 22:21)

"Judas, one of the 12 disciples, had been plotting with Jesus' enemies. For 30 pieces of silver—that was about enough money to buy a suit of clothes—Judas would show them where to capture Jesus that night."

"Did Jesus do anything to stop Judas?" Chris wondered aloud.

"No," Dad replied. "Jesus knew that this plot was part of what was *supposed* to happen that week. Judas left to join Jesus' enemies."

"So what happened next?" asked Chris, leaning his chin on his hands.

"After the Passover dinner, Jesus and His disciples walked to a garden at the foot of the Mount of Olives. The garden was called Gethsemane, which means 'oil press.' Jesus and His disciples loved to visit this spot. That night, though, Jesus was deeply troubled because He knew what was going to happen next. Read what Luke tells us."

[Jesus] withdrew about a stone's throw beyond them, knelt down and prayed, "Father, if You are willing, take this cup from me; yet not my will, but Yours be done."
(Luke 22:41–42)

Chris was puzzled and asked, "If Jesus was God, why would He pray to Himself?"

"Good question!" Dad exclaimed. "Through the miracle of Christmas, God also became a true man in Jesus. The human part of Jesus could suffer, even die—as all humans do—so He prayed for God's help. Keep reading."

When [Jesus] rose from prayer and went back to the disciples, He found them asleep, exhausted from sorrow. (Luke 22:45)

Chris demanded, "*Why* didn't they stay awake? *I* would have!"

"People went to bed just after dark in those days, Chris," said Mom. "They had no electric lights, so this was *late* for them. Besides, the disciples had no idea what a terrible time Jesus was having—and would have later."

"Okay. But what happened to that … traitor Judas?"

"Funny you should ask," said Dad. "Judas then marched into the garden leading a group of armed men from the temple guard. Judas had told them, 'The man I kiss will be Jesus. Seize Him!' "

"Judas *kissed* Jesus? Yecchh!" muttered Chris.

Mom smiled. "In those days a kiss was a way to greet someone," she explained. "This kiss would let the soldiers know which man was Jesus. After all, Jesus' picture would never have appeared on TV or in a newspaper."

"After the kiss, the guards bound Jesus and marched Him off to a hearing before the Jewish Sanhedrin or Council," Dad continued. "Although it was late at night, the high priest—Joseph Caiaphas—and the Council held a trial. They declared Jesus guilty of blasphemy for claiming to be the Son of God and sentenced Him to death. Then they had to take Jesus before the Roman governor to get the death sentence carried out."

"Why?" Chris asked.

"The Romans had final control in Judea—including all cases involving the death penalty," Dad answered. "The Roman governor had to be the one to carry out the execution."

"It was now the day we Christians would later call Good Friday because, on that day, Jesus won our salvation. The Council brought Jesus before Pontius Pilate, the Roman governor, and accused Him of trying to overthrow the government. Pilate quickly saw that the accusation wasn't true. When he found out that Jesus came from Galilee, he decided to send Him to Herod, the ruler of Galilee, who was in Jerusalem celebrating the Passover."

"What a run-around," said Chris. "Wait a minute! Didn't the Wise Men visit Herod when Jesus was just a baby? That Herod must have been *really* old."

"No, no!" said Dad. "This was Herod *Antipas*, the son of the Herod the Magi visited. Antipas was delighted that Pilate had sent Jesus to him. He wanted Jesus to perform a miracle. Herod wanted a magic show, but Jesus kept silent.

"So Herod and his soldiers made fun of Jesus, then sent Him back to Pilate," Dad continued. "Now Pilate had to make a decision, and he decided that the case against Jesus was too weak. He wanted to set Jesus free, but the crowd began to shout, *'Crucify Him! Crucify Him!'* Pilate knew that Jesus wasn't really guilty, so he washed his hands, showing that he was giving up all responsibility for what happened to Jesus."

"Wait a minute," said Chris. "Why would the same people who cheered wildly when Jesus rode by on Palm Sunday now scream *'Crucify Him'* just five days later?"

"Good question," Dad responded. "But these are two different crowds. The people yelling 'crucify' worked at the temple and were controlled by the religious leaders who hated Jesus. Those who had cheered Jesus on Palm Sunday probably didn't even realize He was on trial until after Pilate condemned Him."

"How do you know everyone didn't want to crucify Him?" Chris asked.

"Let's look at what St. Luke wrote for the answer to that question. The soldiers made Jesus carry the beam for His cross to Golgotha—the 'Place of the Skull'— where He would be crucified. Here, listen."

A large number of people followed Him, including women who mourned and wailed for Him. (Luke 23:27)

"That means the Jewish followers of Jesus were *weeping* as He carried His cross to Golgotha," Dad pointed out. "Some people may think that all His countrymen hated Jesus, but this verse shows that it isn't true."

Chris listened carefully as his dad began filling in the details of the crucifixion.

"The soldiers made fun of Jesus—they mocked Him, dressed Him in a robe, and put a crown of thorns on His head. Pilate even placed a sign on the cross that read JESUS OF NAZARETH, THE KING OF THE JEWS. Then they hung Him on the cross."

Chris interrupted. "Why did they hang people on crosses, Dad?"

"Crucifixion was punishment for serious crimes. It was like an advertisement for everyone to see that came with a terrible message: *Don't do what this man did or the same will happen to you!* It was supposed to prevent crime."

"But Jesus was *not* a criminal!" Chris almost shouted. "He was innocent!"

"Exactly! Now you are beginning to understand the real sacrifice of Jesus' death," said Dad. "Just as innocent lambs were sacrificed in the Old Testament, here the Lamb of God Himself was laying down His life. He was taking the punishment for our sins— the greatest example of love the world had ever seen—or would *ever* see."

Chris walked to the window and gazed at the mountain peaks, plated in gold from the setting sun. "Even then Jesus showed His love for everyone, Chris," Mom said quietly. "Here is what He said from the cross."

[Jesus] said, "Father, forgive them, for they do not know what they are doing." (Luke 23:34)

"Two thieves were crucified with Jesus, one on each side," Mom continued. "One taunted Jesus, just like the crowd was doing. The other thief scolded him, saying that they deserved their punishment, but Jesus did not deserve His. Listen to what happened next."

Then [the thief] said, "Jesus, remember me when You come into Your kingdom." Jesus answered him, "Today you will be with me in paradise." (Luke 23:42–43)

Chris looked out at the deepening shadows and asked, "Wasn't there some kind of darkness, Mom?"

"Yes, there was. Jesus was crucified before noon on Good Friday. But from noon until about 3 P.M., darkness covered the entire land."

"Was it an eclipse?" asked Chris. "Like the one we had a couple of years ago?"

"It was probably even darker because this was no eclipse," Dad commented. "The sun and moon were simply in the wrong positions. It seems that the darkness was visible even as far away as the area we call Turkey today."

"Awesome!" Chris said as he came back to the table. "Was that when Jesus died?"

His father nodded and set the Bible in front of Chris. "Why don't you read the very last words of Jesus?" he suggested. Chris read the words slowly and carefully.

Jesus called out with a loud voice, "Father, into Your hands I commit my spirit." When He had said this, He breathed His last. (Luke 23:46)

"Where did they bury Jesus?" Chris asked quietly.

"There was a member of the Jewish Council who had not agreed with the decision to kill Jesus," said Dad. "His name was Joseph of Arimathea. He took Jesus' body off the cross, wrapped it in a linen shroud, and buried Him inside his own new tomb in Jerusalem. Then he rolled a stone in front of the entrance and left."

Christopher crossed his arms on the table, lost in thought.

"But, thank God, that's not the end of the story—at least not *this* story," continued Dad. "Good Friday was followed by Saturday, which many Christians call Easter Vigil. Jesus was dead, but the priests asked Pilate to post guards outside the tomb so His body would not be stolen."

Chris was shocked. "Who would want to steal a *dead* body?"

"Well, maybe the disciples would—*if* they wanted to make the claim later that Jesus had risen from the dead," Dad suggested.

"But the disciples were hiding, terrified for their very lives," Mom objected.

"True enough! But that's what the priests *thought* might happen," Dad replied. "To take extra precautions, they placed soldiers in front of the tomb."

He paused, then added, "Those troops were in for *some* surprise! Here, Chris, start reading chapter 24, where Luke tells about some Galilean women who came to the tomb on Sunday morning to finish preparing Jesus' body for burial. Their names were Mary Magdalene, Joanna, and Mary the mother of James."

Chris read slowly and distinctly, sensing how important the passage was.

On the first day of the week, very early in the morning, the women took the spices they had prepared and went to the tomb. They found the stone rolled away from the tomb, but when they entered, they did not find the body of the Lord Jesus. While they were wondering about this, suddenly two men in clothes that gleamed like lightning stood beside them. In their fright the women bowed down with their faces to the ground, but the men said to them, "Why do you look for the living among the dead? He is not here; He has risen." (Luke 24:1–6a)

"The two men were angels announcing that Jesus had come back to life," Dad explained. "Jesus had actually *risen from the dead*. What He had done for the young man of Nain, He now did for Himself. He was victorious over death so that all believers could have eternal victory in heaven. And to prove that He was truly alive, Jesus appeared many different times, in many different places, over the next 40 days."

"Like where?" Chris asked, once again alive with questions.

"Well, that evening His disciples were huddled together in fear behind locked doors when Jesus suddenly appeared," Dad began.

"Whoa! How did He get in if the doors were locked?" interrupted Chris.

"Locks no longer stopped Jesus," Dad explained. "He could appear and disappear because of His divine nature."

Chris looked startled. "So He was a *ghost* then?"

Dad chuckled and said, "That's exactly what the disciples thought. But to prove that He wasn't a ghost, Jesus ate some fish and invited them to touch Him. Read what He told them."

"Why are you troubled, and why do doubts rise in your minds? Look at my hands and my feet. It is I myself. Touch me and see; a ghost doesn't have flesh and bones, as you see I have." (Luke 24:38–39)

"But if Jesus had a solid body and wasn't a ghost, how did He get through the walls?" Chris asked once more.

"Well, Jesus was both God and man. As God, He could walk through walls. As man, He could eat food. Now does it make more sense?"

Chris rubbed his forehead. "I … I think so. But, you know, it *is* kind of hard to believe."

"Of course it is," Dad agreed. "In fact, even one of Jesus' own disciples didn't even believe it at first. Thomas had not been with the other disciples that night. When they told him that they had seen Jesus, Thomas said, 'No way! I will *not* believe unless I see and touch the nail marks in His hands, and put my finger into the wound in His side!'"

"Did Thomas ever believe?" Chris asked.

"And how! Read what happened when Jesus appeared again a week later."

Though the doors were locked, Jesus came and stood among them and said, "Peace be with you!" Then He said to Thomas, "Put your finger here; see my hands. Reach out your hand and put it into my side. Stop doubting and believe." Thomas said to Him, "My Lord and my God!" (John 20:26–28)

"Jesus also appeared at other times and places, Chris," said Mom. "Luke describes how Jesus joined two of His followers as they walked to a town near Jerusalem called Emmaus. At first they did not recognize Jesus, but they realized who He was as He broke the bread."

"We also read in the gospel of John that Jesus appeared to Mary Magdalene at the tomb and to Simon Peter and the disciples at the Sea of Galilee," Dad added. "And in 1 Corinthians, chapter 15, St. Paul writes that Jesus appeared to more than 500 people at one time. And, yes, He even appeared to Paul himself, who wrote about Jesus' resurrection only 20 years after the first Easter."

"When did Jesus appear to St. Paul?" asked Chris.

"At first his name was Saul and he was not a believer; instead, he persecuted Christians everywhere," Dad replied. "One day, he was on his way to Damascus to persecute the Christians there. Jesus appeared to him in a bright light and spoke to him. After that, Paul believed."

"By that time, of course, Jesus had already ascended into heaven," Mom commented. "Forty days after His resurrection, Jesus gathered His disciples on the Mount of Olives outside Jerusalem. After blessing them, Jesus was lifted up—"

"Yes, I think I know about His sension … ascension, I mean," Chris interrupted. "But how did that work? Didn't it get cold for Jesus as He gained altitude? How did He breathe? How long could the disciples see Him? Did He get smaller and smaller as He shot upward—like the space shuttle?"

Chris stopped to take a breath.

"No, Chris," said Mom. "The gospels tell us that Jesus was hidden by a cloud. This means that, because of His divine nature, Jesus moved into a higher dimension of reality—beyond our human ability to see."

"Now *that* makes sense!" said Chris, looking at his stack of books about space adventures and warp speeds.

"Even *this* is not the end of the story, Chris!" Dad said. "Before ascending into heaven, Jesus promised to be with us always. His great work for us continues. Today He comes to us through the Holy Spirit in Baptism, when we listen to God's Word, and when we receive the Lord's Supper. And we can tell others the Good News of salvation—how all believers will live again in the great resurrection at the end of time, joining Jesus eternally in heaven."

The family devotions had come to end, but Chris sat quietly and reflected on his father's words. "That's a *very important* story!" he said softly.

"How true!" said Mom. "In fact, we thought that it was so important that we named you after Jesus."

Chris' head shot up. He looked from Mom to Dad. "But my name is *Christopher*, not *Jesus*!" he said. "Wasn't I named for Christopher Columbus?"

"No, no," Dad answered with a smile. "Both you and Columbus were named for Jesus Christ. You see, the name *Christopher* means 'bearer of Christ.' Your name proclaims to everyone that you carry the very name of Christ with you wherever you go."

"Awesome!" whispered Chris, delighted with his special link to the very first Easter.

That night, before falling asleep, Christopher gazed at the golden imprint of his name on the cover of the new Bible his parents had given him as an Easter gift.

True stories certainly *were* better than myths or fairy tales. And *this story* would last forever!

Christopher
"bearer of Christ"
Happy Easter!
Love
Mom
and Dad